START-UP
ART AND DESIGN
•••••••••••••••••••••••••••••••••

SELF-PORTRAIT

Louise and Richard Spilsbury

Cherrytree Books are distributed in the
United States by Black Rabbit Books
P.O. Box 3263
Mankato, MN, 56002

Library of Congress Cataloging-in-Publication Data

Spilsbury, Louise.
  Self-portrait / Louise and Richard Spilsbury. -- 1st ed.
    p. cm. -- (Start-up art and design)
  Includes index.
  Summary: "Explores how artists use colors, textures,
and expression to communicate something about
themselves. Includes project ideas for kids to make their
own self-portraits using various techniques"--Provided
by publisher.
  ISBN 978-1-84234-524-5
  1. Self-portraits--Juvenile literature. 2. Art--
Technique--Juvenile literature. I. Spilsbury, Richard,
1963- II. Title.
  N7618.S65 2009
  743.4'2--dc22
                                 2007046391

13-digit ISBN: 9781842345245
10-digit ISBN: 1842345249

First Edition
9 8 7 6 5 4 3 2 1

First published in 2007 by Evans Brothers Ltd.
2A Portman Mansions, Chiltern Street,
London W1U 6NR, United Kingdom

Produced for Evans Brothers Limited by
White-Thomson Publishing Ltd.

Editor: Rachel Minay
Consultant: Susan Ogier Horwood
Designer: Leishman Design

Acknowledgments:
Special thanks to Ms. J. Arundell and pupils at Mayfield
Primary School, Hanwell, West London, for their help
and involvement in the preparation of this book.

Picture Acknowledgments:
Bridgeman Art Library pp. 4l (Giraudon), 8, 14r
(Giraudon); Corbis pp. 4r (Francis G. Mayer), 5l (ROB
& SAS), 5r (image100), 13 (Gianni Dagli Orti); Chris
Fairclough pp. cover tr & main, title page, 6, 7, 10, 11l,
12t, 17l, 18l, 19tl, 20t&b, 21; iStockphoto.com pp. cover
tl, 16 (all).

Artwork:
Pupils at Mayfield Primary School, Hanwell, West
London pp. 9r, 12b (all), 18r, 17r; Tabitha Halliday, age
6, pp. 11r, 15; Emelia Halliday, age 7, p. 14l; Rachel
Minay pp. 19tr, 19bl&r; Robert Sheppard, age 7, p. 9l.

Contents

What Is a Self-Portrait?

Self-portraits are pictures people make of themselves. Self-portraits can tell us what artists look like, or about their lives or feelings.

What do these self-portraits tell you about the artists?

self-portraits   artists

What is special about you? How would you show yourself in a self-portrait?

"I would paint a picture of me with my grandmother. She looks like me."

"I would do a self-portrait of me playing soccer with my best friend."

special

Pencil Self-Portraits

Some self-portraits show only the artist's face.

▲ Compare **your face with a friend's.**
What is different and what is the same?

compare   shading   tones

hading is when you use
ne color to make light
nd dark tones.

▶ Look in a
mirror. Where
re the dark
nd light areas
n your face?

"Part of my
face is in
shadow."

ght

slightly
dark

very
dark

◀ How hard must
you press a pencil
to draw shades
like this?

mirror   shadow

Planning a Portrait

◀ Queen Elizabeth I of England always dressed up for her portrait. She wore jewels and expensive clothes to show she was rich and powerful

What will you wear in your self-portrait? What does the style you choose say about you?

portrait   style

What **props** will you include? Artists show their **identity**
in the objects or people they put in their self-portraits.

What do these self-portraits tell us?

props   identity

Paint Effects

Clare's class uses brushes and other objects to create different **textures** with paint.

"I'm using a comb to show the texture of my hair."

textures   experiment

▼ The children experiment with colors. They mix paints to make a skin tone that closely matches their own. What colors would you mix to make your skin tone?

▲ Tabitha mixed paint to match her skin tone, then added her features with other media. What do you think she used?

Tip: Look after your equipment. Wash brushes and pack paints away afterward.

features   media

Mood Pictures

► Chandra's class reads *The Owl Who Was Afraid of the Dark*. The children discuss fear and other emotions.

▼ What emotions do these mood pictures show?

emotions   mood

This artist used color and swirling paint textures to express his mood. Does his facial expression tell you how he is feeling?

Chandra's class thinks of colors to suggest different moods.

angry

peaceful

sad

happy

thoughtful

facial expression

Symbolic Art

► **This portrait of a pharaoh includes symbols with special meanings. The eye represents perfection.**

◄ **Emelia drew herself in profile. How else is her picture similar to the pharaoh's?**

ome self-portraits don't show people at all. They use
ymbols to show the artist's personality.

◄ Draw around
your hand and
color it in.
Fill the spaces
with images
that say
something
about you.

profile   personality   images   15

Life-size Collage

A **collage** is made by sticking paper and other **materials** on to a flat surface. Maya's class draws **outlines** of each other to make **life-size** self-portraits.

Match these adjectives to the materials Maya collected

furry   shiny   smooth   bumpy   soft   silky

collage   materials   outlines

The children rip paper and cut fabric to make different-sized pieces for their collage.

"I braided this wool to make soft hair."

life-size   adjectives   fabric

Photo Faces

Amir's class takes digital photos of each other. They try different **poses** and **gestures**.

► Sasha made an **alter ego** self-portrait with her photo. Which sides of her personality does it show?

poses   gestures   alter ego

Amir uses an effects tool on the computer to create an unusual self-portrait.

Some children use the computer to overlap lots of different photos. This kind of picture is called a photomontage.

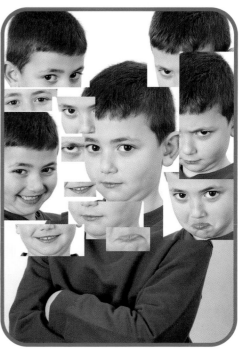

photomontage

On Display

▲ **What do you think frames do to a picture?**

◄ **You could make a colorful frame for your self-portrait. Think about symmetry in your design.**

frames   symmetry

The children review their work. They think about what they would improve or do differently in future.

"Next time, I'll add more texture to my self-portrait."

"I'll include my best friend and my dog in my next self-portrait."

review   improve

Further Information for

Possible Activities

PAGES 4-5

The first self-portrait on page 4 is *Myself, Portrait-Landscape* (1890) by Henri Rousseau. It shows him about to retire from his job as a customs officer and take his place as an artist in Paris. The second image, *Self-portrait with Daughter* (1789) by Élisabeth-Louise Vigée-Le Brun, is much more personal and intimate.

The children could collect family portraits and spot resemblances. Then they could draw how they think they will look when they are adults! They could also draw self-portraits that include family members.

PAGES 6-7

To help the children look more closely you could play a game. One child leaves the room and the others have to describe her or him from memory. Tell me about the way X looks. Can you remember what clothes Y was wearing?

Do a drag and drop activity to draw a portrait online at http://www.mrpicassohead.com/create.html

Children could try drawing pencil portraits without taking the pencil off the paper, or by drawing with their eyes shut, or by drawing with one hand what the other feels as they run their fingers over their face.

PAGES 8-9

Local museums and galleries may do workshops or talks linked to self-portraits. Or you can download information from the National Gallery of Art (http://www.nga.gov/education/classroom/self_portraits) and adapt it to visit your local gallery. Children could research and be inspired by many different artists. A self-portrait inspired by Georges Seurat and pointillism could use ear cleaners to make dots to fill in hair, skin, and clothes. Or children could do a cubist self-portrait inspired by a Picasso.

PAGES 10-11

Children could enlarge their pencil self-portraits on the photocopier and then try out different effects on the copies. They could mix glue and paint and experiment with this and different brushes to create surface patterns and textures.

Parents and Teachers

PAGES 12-13

Children could research the Arcimboldo portraits made using fruit and flowers to show the parts of the face and draw a face of their own using different objects for parts of the face.
The class could explore Picasso's fawn plates. The children could draw self-portraits on paper plates, perhaps even choosing an animal's face to represent them.

PAGES 14-15

Children could do a symbolic self-portrait using images that represent something about them. For example, if they are interested in cooking, they could make a collage with pasta and pictures of food from magazines cut into the shapes of their features.

PAGES 16-17

At http://www.article19.com/shockwave/makeaface.htm there is a drop and drag activity for children to create faces with different moods.
Children could also make clay faces by pressing fingers and tools into the surface of clay, and building up a 3D texture. They could create a number of faces expressing a range of different emotions.
Children could experiment with color using their photocopied line portraits (see notes for pages 10–11). They can try coloring the copies to see how different colors can change a picture's mood. They could also use colored gels or transparencies to change the colors instantly.

PAGES 18-19

After taking a digital photo, use the effect tools in a program such as Paint Shop Pro to make a line or charcoal drawing of the photo. This can be used as an aid to assist with children's portrait drawing. ArtRage is an art package for your computer

Further Information

BOOKS FOR CHILDREN
What Is a Self-Portrait? (Art's Alive!) by Ruth Thompson (Sea to Sea Publications, 2005)
I'm Good at Art (Read & Learn) by Eileen Day (Raintree, 2004)
Line and Tone (How Artists Use...) by Paul Flux (Heinemann Library, 2007)
Pattern and Texture (How Artists Use...) by Paul Flux (Heinemann Library, 2007)

WEB SITES
http://www.fm.coe.uh.edu/resources/portrait_detectives/pd_criteria.html
www.carearts.org/lessons/self_portrait_paper.html
http://pbskids.org/arthur/parentsteachers/activities/acts/self_portrait.html
http://www.tate.org.uk/learning/kids

that is free to download.
Children could research the photomontages of David Hockney and use these as inspiration for their own photomontages.

PAGES 20-21

Frames in galleries celebrate and emphasize artists' paintings and pictures. When children frame their pictures, they could give them a title and date them, too.
A class could arrange a self-portrait competition, either in a gallery or by uploading photos of the class portraits on to the school web site. The children could ask parents to match each child's name to his or her self-portrait.

23

Index